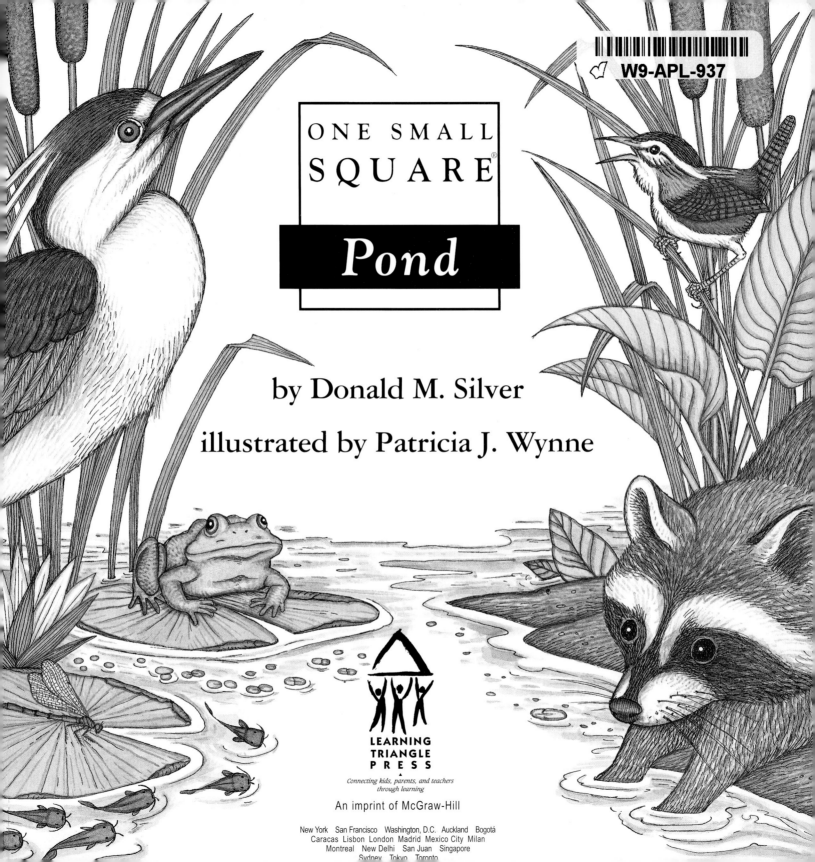

ONE SMALL SQUARE®

Pond

by Donald M. Silver

illustrated by Patricia J. Wynne

LEARNING
TRIANGLE
PRESS

*Connecting kids, parents, and teachers
through learning*

An imprint of McGraw-Hill

New York   San Francisco   Washington, D.C.   Auckland   Bogotá
Caracas   Lisbon   London   Madrid   Mexico City   Milan
Montreal   New Delhi   San Juan   Singapore
Sydney   Tokyo   Toronto

Every plant and animal pictured in this book can be found with its name on pages 38–43. If you come to a word you don't know or can't pronounce, look for it on pages 44–47. The small diagram of a square on some pages shows the distance above or below the water for that section of the book.

For Elaine Ribando

who always made us laugh

Many thanks to Dr. Melanie Stiassny of the American Museum of Natural History, Karen Malkus, Ivy Sky Rutzky, Maceo Mitchell, and Thomas L. Cathey for their encouragement and valued contributions to this book. Special thanks to Dr. Elizabeth Ann Gammon for a tour of ponds in southern Illinois. We are forever indebted to Jackie Bell for putting the foundation under our castle in the air.

ISBN 0-07-057932-6
1 2 3 4 5 6 7 8 9 QPD/QPD 9 0 2 1 0 9 8 7

Whether you are outside or at home, always obey safety rules! Neither the publisher nor the author shall be liable for any damage that may be caused or any injury sustained as a result of doing any of the activities in this book.

Introduction

Sometimes nature tricks people. Take a pond, for instance. How peaceful it always looks! A large bird may be standing in the water without moving a muscle. Nearby a turtle pokes its head through the reeds. A lazy frog basking on a lily pad barely glances at what looks like a raft made of jelly floating by. Under the water a fish swims back and forth.

The only sound is the whirring of a dragonfly's wings. Even the water is still. Now that's a sure sign nothing much is going on, right?

Nothing much is going on! Tell that to the fish about to be speared by the bird's long, sharp beak. Or to the frog that may become the turtle's next meal. That jelly raft is filled with eggs, each of which has a tiny tadpole growing.

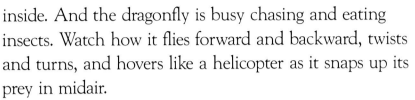

inside. And the dragonfly is busy chasing and eating insects. Watch how it flies forward and backward, twists and turns, and hovers like a helicopter as it snaps up its prey in midair.

A pond is home to more creatures doing more things than you ever imagined. Explore a pond and you will discover so much happening that you will wonder how you might have thought differently. Just wait until you see what is living on the underside of a lily pad—or in a drop of pond water.

There are millions of ponds all over the world, so you have a good chance of finding one near home. It might be in a park, the woods, or a meadow—or even in a neighbor's backyard. If the pond is on someone else's land, you must get the owner's permission to explore it. Otherwise, all you need is simple equipment, as shown on this page.

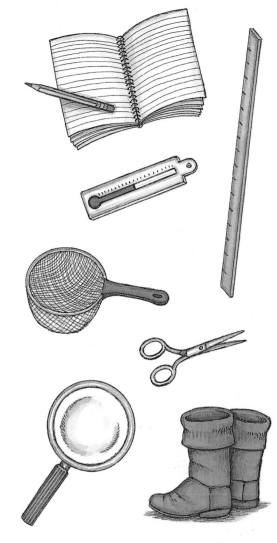

What's Living in a Pond?

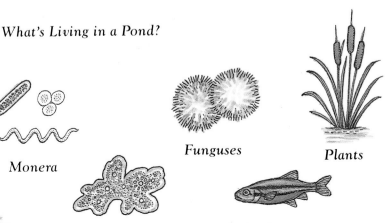

Monera

Funguses

Protists

Animals

Plants

With simple equipment you can get a close-up look at how many of the plants and animals in your small square "make their living" there. Wear old clothes and sneakers or boots to walk and sit on any wet ground around the pond.

Safety First

1. Tell an ADULT where you are going.
2. Be careful NOT TO SLIP at the pond's edge.
3. DO NOT go into the water. You don't know where it may become dangerously deep.
4. NEVER drink pond water. You don't know what's in it.
5. STAY OFF any piers that extend into the water.

Measuring Up

To measure your small square, stand a footstep away from the water's edge. Take a yardstick or a meterstick (about three inches longer) and draw a line 24 inches (61 cm) long in the earth or mud with a twig.

Next, stand at either end of the line. Hold one hand over the 24-inch mark on the yardstick (61-cm mark on the meterstick) and extend the long part over the water as shown. NEVER try to reach farther with your hands or tools.

Now, hold one end of the stick and lower the other into the water as shown. If the water is deeper than 6 inches (15 cm), move to another spot and start again.

1 FOOTSTEP

LINE IN THE MUD

24 INCHES

24 INCHES

DIPS NO MORE THAN 6 INCHES

One Small Square of a Pond

You may already have your eye on a pond near home that you want to explore. If so, walk around it a few times. Choose a spot on the shore where you can sit, stand, and reach over the water's edge without danger of falling in.

If you don't know of any ponds nearby, ask at home or at the library. There may be one closer than you think. If not, let this book be your pond for now. Perhaps sometime soon you will get to visit a pond.

This book explores only one small square of a pond. That square, shown here, is two feet long on each side — about as big as the seat of an easy chair. As you follow along, there will be activities you can do in the square that will not harm your pond.

Before you go any further, STOP! Read the Safety First column on this page. It will explain how to measure off your small square without stepping into the water.

A pond is an ever-changing world of swimmers, divers, rowers, crawlers, climbers, and skaters. It is where plants grow in, on, and out of water.

No two ponds are exactly the same. So don't expect all the living things in this book to be in your pond. And you may discover many others that "make their living" in ways similar to those in this small square.

Cut cattail stems in your square can mean "muskrat at work." Look for the home it builds out on the water.

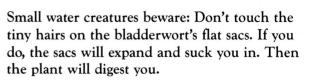

Small water creatures beware: Don't touch the tiny hairs on the bladderwort's flat sacs. If you do, the sacs will expand and suck you in. Then the plant will digest you.

Ducklings, too, may explore your small square.

Freeze! Reach for the sky! With a beak, that is. A bittern hides from danger — pretending it is just another cattail or reed.

What is a flying ferry for fish eggs? A great blue heron that flies from pond to pond with eggs stuck to its legs.

8

Above your square, birds
snap up insects on the wing.

School's Out: Summer's In

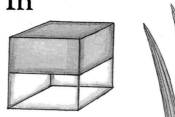

You could start in autumn, when
leaves are falling. Or in winter, when
ice is forming. Or in spring, when
buds are popping. But early summer is perfect time to
begin exploring a pond. By then, days are long and warm.
Most ponds are bursting with life. Visit your square often:
in the morning, at midday, and before sunset.

As you near the pond, a big bullfrog may leap up out
of nowhere and bound off as fast as it can. A bird may
suddenly rise from your square and fly quickly away. Like
all other pond animals, they are on the lookout for
danger. They will flee or hide if they mistake you for a
predator—an animal that wants to eat them. So walk
slowly to your square and try not to make any sounds
that will scare away pond creatures.

Stand on the edge of the line you drew in the earth.
At first glance, you may see nothing but plants growing
out of the shallow water. Soon you will notice that in this

Look for a hole dug into the mud at
the edge of your square. There may
be a crayfish inside.

Fish eggs

9

Your Pond Notebook

Whenever you visit your square,
carry a notebook and a pen or
pencil with you. Record the date,
the time, and the weather. Draw

pictures and take notes of what
pond plants and animals look
like and what they are doing.
Record sounds and smells too.
Soon your notebook will be full
of clues to how a pond works
and how it changes with the
seasons.

Left Behind

You're not the only pond visitor.
Check the mud in and near your
square for tracks left by animals
that came to feed, drink, or hide
from predators.

LITTLE BIRD
WALKING

GREAT BLUE HERON

Get to know the plants growing at the edge of your square by the shape and color of their stems, flowers, and leaves. Look for animals that feed, hide, or lay eggs on them.

A dragonfly lays eggs (1) in a pond. Each egg hatches into a nymph (2) that lives underwater. The nymph climbs out of the water and sheds its skin (3). It is now an adult (4).

part of the pond blackbirds build nests, spiders spin webs, insects flutter in and out, and wrens bob up and down on grassy stems. Here animals crawl out of the water to sun, dig, or even shed their skin right before your eyes. Some hide where their body colors blend into their surroundings.

Gently touch a plant leaf, if you can. In it are millions of cells that capture energy from the sun. With this energy, the cells make food using water from the pond and carbon dioxide gas from the air. During this process, called photosynthesis, the leaves make oxygen gas and release it into the air. As you explore, you are breathing in some of that oxygen.

Listen for the buzz of insects that are attracted to the

Pond water is fresh water, not salty like sea water.

Cattail pollen

Burreed pollen

Not only insects carry pollen from male to female flower parts. So do birds and the wind. Without this help, most plants could not make seeds.

colors and odors of flowers. Watch the insects land and sip sweet-tasting nectar the flowers make.

As the insects sip, they brush against male flower parts that are full of powdery pollen. Some pollen clings to their bodies. When the insects fly to the next flower of the same kind, some pollen drops and lands on female flower parts. Only then can a flower begin to make seeds from which new plants can grow.

If a plant stem is arching over your small square, you may wonder what it is up to. It isn't confused: far from it. It is a water willow, just one of the plants that first grows near shore and then changes direction in order to invade deeper water. Try to guess how far it will reach during the summer before touching down and growing new roots.

Just Ducky

Wood ducks lay eggs in holes in trees that overhang ponds. When the eggs hatch, the babies answer their parents' calls by jumping from the hole into the water below. Not all ponds have trees with holes over the water. Try to attract wood ducks to your pond by giving them a place to nest.

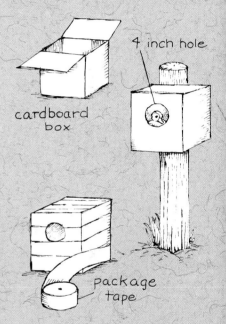

4 inch hole

cardboard box

package tape

Find an empty cardboard box about a foot long on each side. Cut a hole four inches in diameter, as shown. Wrap the box in plastic package tape, leaving the hole open. This will waterproof the box. Tie the box to a piece of wood, as shown. Stick the wood firmly in the muddy bottom at the edge of the pond away from your square. Do not disturb the box even if you see a wood duck fly into it. One day you may find baby wood ducks swimming in your square.

These spiders have no need for a web. When the water moves, they can sense if it is dinnertime.

Between Two Worlds

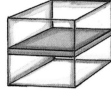

At first you may not believe your eyes. So just keep watching the surface of the water in your square. Soon your doubts will disappear.

Yes, bugs *are* skating on the pond. Something *does* keep making dimples in the surface. An animal with eight legs *is* running on the water. Not one of these creatures ever gets its feet wet!

The pond skaters are water striders. The dimple makers are springtails. The runner is a fisher spider hunting insects. All of them are held up by an invisible, elastic "film" that forms because the water surface stretches and pulls itself tight.

You're not seeing double. The whirligig beetle is, with two eyes on each side. As one peers above water, the other peers below.

Look for duckweed floating on your square. It is one of the smallest flowering plants on earth. Ducks can't eat enough of it.

Duckweed

Water strider leg

Surface film

Your hand can easily break through the film. Go ahead, try it. The film can't stop a turtle or a frog from entering the water either.

Do you see any little black tops spinning in circles? These are whirligig beetles. They break through the surface film too. But they spin with their bodies half in the water and half out.

Springtails are so lightweight that they only dent the film as they hop across the water. Water striders and fisher spiders are also light. They spread their weight over their long legs, and feathery hairs on their feet push water away. The surface film supports these creatures, keeping them in the world of air above and out of the world of water below.

WATCH OUT! The water snakes where you live may be poisonous. Even if they are not, most water snakes bite.

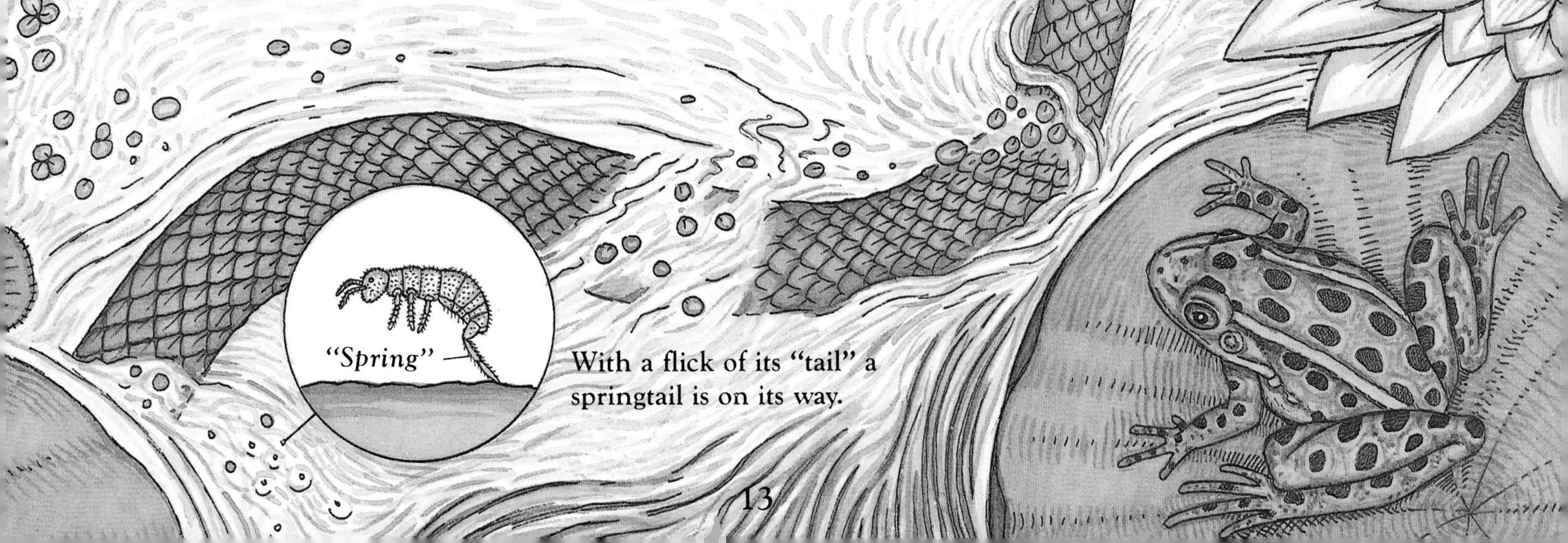

"Spring"

With a flick of its "tail" a springtail is on its way.

The Hangout

Mosquito eggs float on the water. They hatch into larvas that grow and change into comma-shaped pupas. An adult mosquito pushes out of the pupa and flies off to feed and mate.

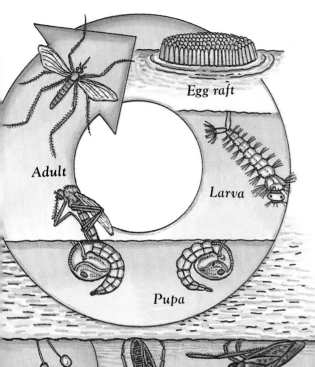

Egg raft

Adult

Larva

Pupa

First comes the bite. Then comes the itch. Before you can say "Gotcha!" you've been bitten again. That settles it: Mosquitoes are back in force.

You have probably been staring, without knowing it, at rafts of mosquito eggs floating in your square. From each egg hatches a tiny mosquito larva. It lives and grows in the water until it changes into an adult and flies off.

Finding food is no trouble for a mosquito larva. But breathing is. A mosquito larva can get its oxygen only from the air. It cannot absorb oxygen from the water, as fishes can. So what does it do? It hangs upside down in the water from the surface film. Then the larva pokes a tube through the film and breathes in air just like a swimmer wearing a snorkel.

Midge eggs

Like all living things, water plants and animals make carbon dioxide gas as a waste product and release it into the world around them.

There are about a hundred reasons why this giant male water bug has come up for air. Those are the eggs that a female has cemented on his back. For a week, until the eggs hatch, he must make sure they get plenty of oxygen.

The hydra doesn't need air, just a place to hang with its tentacles stretched out. Armed with stinging cells, the tentacles catch prey.

Mosquito larvas aren't the only animals that hang from the film. Rat-tailed maggots and water scorpions may be there too, with their own "snorkels." So may an upside-down snail, which moves along like a fly walking on a ceiling.

Then there are water boatmen, backswimmers, and diving beetles. These insects are always busy hunting underwater. Because they are also air breathers, they keep returning to the surface film. The only way they can stay underwater is to carry their own air supply with them. At the surface they trap air bubbles under their wing covers, under their wings, or at the rear of their bodies. When they run out of air, they must dart back up to the film and hang out again.

Snail eggs

Not only plants need the sun. So do water animals. Without the sun's energy, pond water would be too cold for them.

For a water flea the surface film is the place to hang out and snack on pollen that has fallen onto the water.

That Sinking Feeling

A lily pad floats. So does a twig. But a rock you drop in the pond sinks. Water pushes up on the lily pad and twig, keeping them afloat. It also pushes up on the rock, but not with enough force to keep the rock from sinking. The rock is so heavy for its size that it overcomes the push of the water.

Fill a bowl with water and try to predict, from their size, weight, and shape, whether the following will sink or float: a paper clip, a button, a piece of paper, a pin, a bottle cap, a coin, a ball of cotton, a rubber band. Try others, too.

Where Is It?

Place a coin in an empty bowl. Move the bowl until the coin is just out of sight. Slowly fill the cup with water. What happens? Now reach for the coin. Is it where you think it is? Light bends when it passes from air to water. It makes the coin appear to be where it isn't. The same is true for pond life. It may seem to be in a certain spot—but is it?

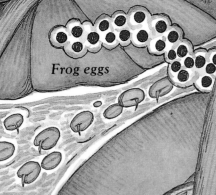

Frog eggs

The milky blob isn't one
moss animal but a colony—
many together. If the colony
moves four inches in a day, it
is moving fast.

Moss
animal
colony

Baby fishes try to avoid
predators by swimming
under lily pads.

Everyone wants to get in
on the act. A blue
damselfly sticks her tail
underwater and lays eggs
on the lily stem.

Leaf beetle e

Snail
eggs

Out of Sight

When you look at a lily pad, what do you see? A green leaf? Of course. The food maker for the lily plant? Certainly. A sundeck for a spotted newt? Perhaps. A heliport for dragonflies? Definitely. A floating dining room where a frog can sit and snatch insects out of the air with its long, sticky tongue? That too.

Just when you think the list is complete, along comes a coot. This black bird steps onto a lily pad and uses its short white beak to pull an edge of the pad out of the water. The coot isn't interested in the part of the leaf you can see. It is after what is on the flip side. To the coot a lily pad is a restaurant that is out of sight.

What a menu: snails, worms, water bugs, and small fishes to delight any hungry coot. There are also clams and sponges, hydras and water mites, and lots and lots of eggs. Indeed, dozens of kinds of creatures live under a lily pad. There they are close to the surface yet shaded from the sun and hidden from many pond predators.

If there is a lily pad near you, dip you fingers into the water and sprinkle some on top of the pad. A thin waxy coating pushes the water away. The water forms beads that do not wet the leaf or clog tiny breathing holes in it. Instead, when the wind blows, the beads just run off.

The underside of a lily pad has no breathing holes. It isn't waxy and doesn't push the water away. It hugs the water and resists being turned over. That helps all the creatures living there to stay out of sight.

Leaf It Up

Pond creatures live under any floating leaf. If you can safely reach a lily pad or other floater with your hand or yardstick, pull it in and cut it from its stem. Place the cut leaf in a white enamel pan and cover the leaf with water. Turn the leaf over and look at it with your magnifying glass. In your notebook, draw everything you see, including the leaf. When you are finished, pour the leaf and the water back into the pond. The creatures will soon find another leafy shelter.

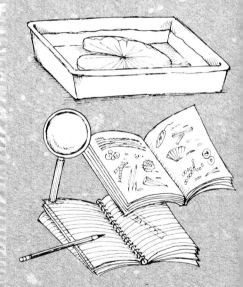

A field guide can help you identify what you have seen under the leaf. A field guide is a book with the names and pictures of animals and plants that live in different places. There are guides for insects, birds, fishes—just about everything in nature, even ponds. You may have field guides at home. If not, you can find them at the library.

Quite a Handful

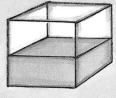

Scoop up some pond water in your hand. Now, what are you holding? Sounds like a trick question, doesn't it? Well, it is.

You *are* holding a handful of water. But you are also holding the keys to life in a pond. In your hand are thousands of food makers and creatures that eat them.

Look closely at the water. You may see some greenish threads or some tiny moving blobs. But you will not see the living things as shown on these pages even if they are in your hands. To see them you would have to look through a microscope. And everything here—and more—would fit in just one drop of water.

Imagine a drop of pond water magnified to more than 700 times its normal size. These living things would be only this big.

Algae and plants turn the sun's energy into chemical energy that is stored in the food they make. Animals use this chemical energy to grow and move.

Yellow-green pond water is a clue that the number of algae is skyrocketing. Most algae divide by splitting in two.

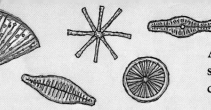

All the tiny living things that swim or drift in the water are called plankton.

Most of the living things in a drop of pond water are algae. Algae have no leaves, stems, or roots. But like water lilies and other plants, algae make food using energy from the sun. And they also make oxygen.

The food made by the algae is passed along to the tiny creatures, small fishes, insect larvas, and clams that eat the algae. Then large fishes, snapping turtles, herons, and other predators hunt the smaller pond animals.

Without algae there would soon be no food in the pond for most animals. Without the oxygen that algae make, fishes and other underwater breathers would soon use up all the oxygen the pond absorbs from the air.

Food, oxygen, water, algae—the keys to pond life. All in one drop. All in your hand.

A paramecium becomes a meal for an amoeba. Another divides in two. One life ends and another takes its place.

Green algae

Besides drifting in pond water, algae also grow in stems, rocks, shells—anywhere they can.

Amoeba

Paramecium

19

Risky Business

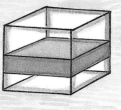

After a few visits to your small square, you expect to see a turtle or a frog climb out of the pond. You aren't surprised when mosquitoes and other insects fly up from the water surface. If a "periscope" rises from the middle of your square, that's another story. You have every right to wonder what on earth is going on underwater.

In an instant the mystery is solved. The "periscope" is attached to the body of a bird, not to a minisubmarine. It is the head and neck of a pied-billed grebe, a shy bird that may call your pond home.

It's fun to count how many seconds the grebe can stay

One pickerel lurking under the lily pads will chase all other pickerels from your square.

Nearly all moths live only on land. But not this little brown moth breaking out of its underwater cocoon.

Air bubble

The water spider makes its web a bubble home by filling it with air. This spider is found in Europe and Asia.

20

underwater before it must come up for air. Or to try to predict where in the pond the "periscope" will reappear after each dive. Just keep in mind that the grebe isn't diving for fun. It is a predator that makes its living hunting insects, fishes, snails, and crayfishes.

The grebe isn't the only underwater hunter in your square. You've already seen others darting up to the surface film to "tank up" on air bubbles. That giant water bug that caught your eye heads back to the hunt by rowing its legs like oars. The diving beetle biting a fish or a tadpole is really injecting a poison that turns the prey's insides into a soupy delight for dinner.

One predator in your square, the dragonfly nymph, just can't seem to get its fill of food. It looks as if it is wear-

The chase is on. Each pond creature must eat without being eaten.

What a change from egg (1) to tadpole (2) to adult frog (3). A tadpole looks, swims, and breathes like a fish. It eats plants and algae. An adult can live and breathe on land.

Gills

Fishes breathe through gills, not lungs. Through gills fishes take in oxygen from the water and give off carbon dioxide.

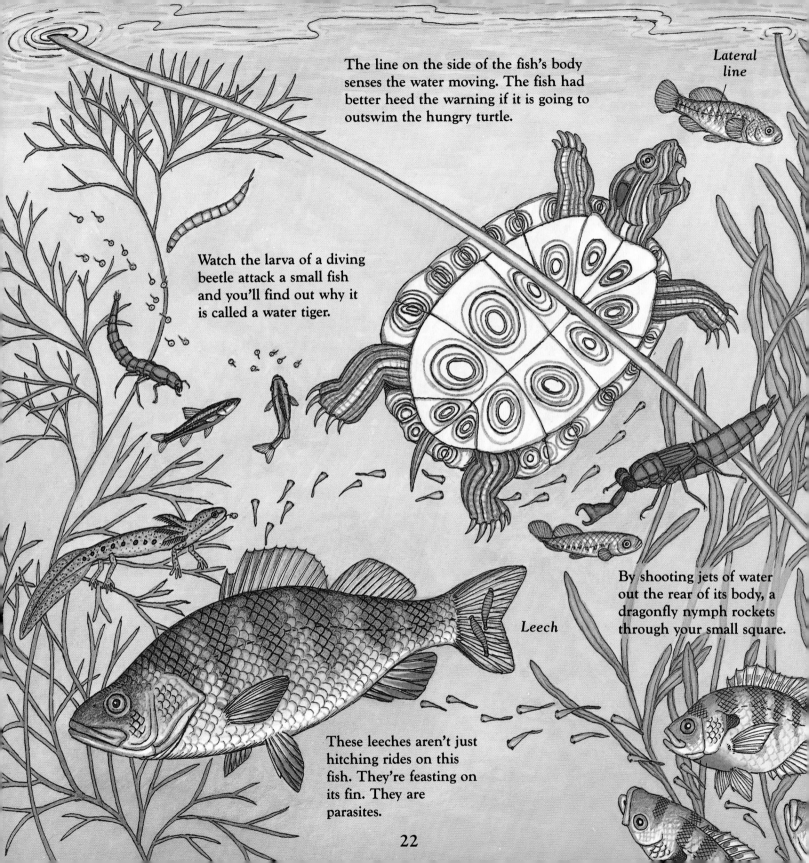

The line on the side of the fish's body senses the water moving. The fish had better heed the warning if it is going to outswim the hungry turtle.

Lateral line

Watch the larva of a diving beetle attack a small fish and you'll find out why it is called a water tiger.

By shooting jets of water out the rear of its body, a dragonfly nymph rockets through your small square.

Leech

These leeches aren't just hitching rides on this fish. They're feasting on its fin. They are parasites.

22

ing a mask. The "mask" is part of the nymph's secret weapon—its long lower lip, folded under its mouth.

As a dragonfly nymph rockets through the water or waits near the pond bottom, it searches for prey. If an unsuspecting fish or tadpole swims by, the nymph shoots out its lip with lightning speed. The prey has no time to escape the sharp hooks on the lip's tip, and the nymph reels in its meal.

It's good for predators that there are so many small fishes, tadpoles, and other prey to eat each day. But it is also good for the pond. Most pond creatures lay thousands of eggs. If all the eggs hatched and grew into adults, there wouldn't be enough food or space for them.

That doesn't mean that predators always have the upper hand. Far from it. Staying alive is risky business for predators as well as prey. Predators can *become* prey. Also, if predators captured all the prey in a pond, they would soon be without food.

Capturing prey is hard work. Some creatures in the pond are transparent, so predators cannot see them. Others have colors or patterns that help camouflage—hide—them. Sponges taste so bad that few predators bother with them. Snails pull into their shells when they sense danger. Fishes try to swim to safety among plant stems or under lily pads.

If all else fails, animals will fight for their lives, using their teeth, muscles, claws, or any other body part they can. It's the risk they have to take.

Square With a View

Why miss out on what's going on underwater when you can make a pond viewer? It will get rid of glare and reflections that make it hard to see.

Cut the top and bottom off an empty milk container, as shown. Cover one cutoff end with clear heavy-duty plastic wrap so that the wrap extends about halfway up the outside of the container. Pull the wrap tight and tape around the sides with waterproof plastic tape.

plastic wrap

tape

Lie flat on the ground at the edge of your square. Carefully lower the end with the wrap into the water. Don't let any water get into the container. Now look inside. Is anything looking back at you?

Bottoming Out

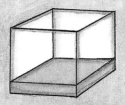

Something is stirring at the bottom of your square. It's the mud. No, it's a fish stirring up the mud with its fins. A male sunfish is clearing a circle for his nest.

When the nest is ready, a female may lay thousands of eggs in it. Then the male will cover them with sperm. A baby fish can develop when a sperm enters an egg.

After laying eggs, the female swims away. But the male stays. His work is just beginning. He must protect the eggs from egg eaters. He must also keep dirt and other particles off the eggs. With his fins he fans water over the eggs to sweep them clean. The moving water also delivers oxygen to the fast-growing babies.

The spongilla sponge lives on a stem. The spongilla fly larva will eat both the sponge and the food the sponge traps.

A patch of red may be tubifex worms wiggling in the mud.

Tubifex worms

Going up! Minerals and water move through tubes from the lily roots to the stem and leaves.

After about five days the eggs hatch. Even then, the male's work is still not done. For a while he will try to keep his family swimming together and safe from predators. Only when the babies are large enough to take care of themselves will the male go his own way.

It's lucky that your square is in shallow water. If sunlight didn't reach to the bottom, you'd miss the sunfish and his nest. You wouldn't be able to watch a bullhead feel for food with the "whiskers" under its chin. And you wouldn't have a front-row seat for the underwater invasion of the pond by plants that send out stems along the bottom to take root in deeper water.

Air spaces in the lily stem help make it light enough to stay up in the water. The spaces also store extra oxygen.

Ready...aim...a mussel shoots its larvas at a fish. The larvas hook on to the fish for a month or so. They feed on the fish and start to turn into adults. Then they unhook, sink, and dig into the mud.

Mussel larva

Stored food

Going down! Food and oxygen move through tubes from the lily leaves to the stem and roots. Some of the food the lily doesn't use it stores for winter.

A snapping turtle doesn't mind spending time down below the surface. It finds not only live animals to capture but also dead creatures that are as tasty to eat.

For the animals in the circle nothing beats swimming, digging, or crawling in the mud. They are well fitted to live there.

Amphipod

Isopod

Tubifex worm

Dinner is always being served to the cleanup crew at the bottom of your square. What they don't eat recyclers break down. Now that's a mouthful.

Just Keep Raining

It's raining. Just what the pond needs: more water to replace all it has lost in the summer heat. The heat speeds up evaporation—liquid water changing into a gas and escaping into the air.

The downpour adds something else to the pond besides water. It washes in dust, dirt, and tiny soil particles, called silt, from the land.

Soon enough the clouds disappear. The rain is over. Or is it? Now the silt, dirt, and dust slowly "rain" down on the pond bottom. So do a leaf the wind blew onto your square, and pollen, and animal droppings. In fact, every day bits of plants and animals rain down on the mud.

This "rain" is just what the pond needs too. In the mud live nature's cleanup crew and recycling team. Worms and other crew members eat some dead plant and animal parts. Bacteria, funguses, and other recyclers break down the rest into nutrients. Without these nutrients, plants and algae could not keep growing and making more food. If the rain were to stop, so would the life of the pond. It had better just keep on raining.

In a teaspoon of mud live millions of bacteria, funguses, and protists. Some can keep recycling even if all the oxygen in the mud is used up.

Bacterium

Protist

Muck It Up

Half fill a white enamel pan with pond water. Lie down at the edge of your square and scoop up some of the muck from the pond bottom with a metal food strainer. Be sure to ask permission to use the strainer first.

Empty the muck into the pan and set the pan in the shade for a while. Then look under your magnifying glass for creatures wiggling, squiggling, twisting, and turning in the muddy water. You may see clams, worms, tiny crayfishes, amphipods on their sides, even a dragonfly nymph. DO NOT pick up any in your hand. Many pond creatures bite. Draw what you see in your notebook. Then pour the muddy water back into your square.

Come and Get It

Tie a piece of raw meat to a string. Lower it into your square until it touches bottom. After ten minues pull it out. Look under your magnifying glass for flatworms and other feeders enjoying the feast.

Ostracods
Midge larva
Amphipod

A red bat zeros in on dinner with sounds too high-pitched for you to hear. They bounce off flying insects and echo back to the bat, leading the bat to its prey.

As the sky darkens, many small creatures rise to the surface from deeper waters. It's feeding time.

Sunset signals sleep for some animals and hunting for others.

Twilight Time

The long summer day is about to end. The sun sets and the air cools. How peaceful the pond seems. Oops! Not that again!

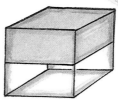

For about an hour the sky will still be light. That's just long enough for you to discover the twilight world of your small square and make it home before darkness falls.

Sit at the edge of your square and listen to the sounds of evening: the deep call of a bullfrog bellowing *chug-o-rum, chug-o-rum* or the hoot of an owl in a nearby tree. Watch for bats skimming the water surface, filling their stomachs with midges and other insects.

The lily flowers are all closed. If you have a flashlight, shine it over your square. Eight bright green dots may be a fisher spider's eyes reflecting your beam. Underwater most fishes are already asleep: open-eyed, because they have no eyelids. Water fleas and other creatures twitching every which way are far from resting.

On shore a crayfish may be digging in the mud. A little shrew may dive into the water, then climb out with a morsel in its mouth. A raccoon may dip in its paws and grab what it can to eat. Remember: These are wild animals, so keep your distance.

Above, a spring peeper frog calls for a mate. Below, a crayfish digs a tunnel from land to water as an escape or a hiding place.

Heeding the Warning

Don't clear away leaves that fall in the water. When they sink, they will decay and add nutrients that pond plants need to grow.

By late August you can tell that the days are much shorter and the nights much cooler. Pond life can tell too. These changes signal that winter is on its way. In places where winter is bitterly cold, there is no time to waste. Each kind of living thing needs protection from freezing to death. Visit your square as summer turns into autumn and you will discover how nature goes about doing that.

Nearly all the pond birds take off and fly toward places where winters are warm. Like you and other mammals, birds make their own body heat. But the energy for making heat comes from food. Before their food supply runs out, the birds are on their way to their warm winter feeding grounds.

It's that arching water willow again! Just when other plants are dying, it is flowering.

"Wintering" sponge

"Wintering" moss animal

"Wintering" rotifer

Before the frost, rotifers, moss animals, and sponges die. But first they form eggs or balls of cells that will start growing in spring.

30

None of the insects, fishes, or other water animals can make their own body heat. Plants can't either. When the air or water chills, so do they. But they cannot follow the birds to warmer places.

Explore your square as summer ends and you will find fewer and fewer creatures. Many have been eaten by predators. Others have died soon after mating. But those that remain aren't moving as fast as they once did. It takes them longer and longer to get their muscles working now that the sun's rays deliver less warmth to your square. There is less and less food to be found.

Many plants are disappearing. The lily flowers break apart. The lily pads sink. Leaves on other plants blow into the water. Stems wither. Before the frost the pond will be ready for winter.

The clear water is a clue that your square in autumn is less rich in algae.

Feel the water and you will know why turtles and frogs move a lot slower now than they did in summer.

A water strider waits out winter in the earth at the water's edge.

Some algae make oxygen all winter. But most oxygen comes from the air. If pond ice does not crack after a few weeks pond animals may die from a lack of oxygen.

In some places it is so cold that ponds do freeze from top to bottom. However, the mud still protects the creatures in it.

Thin Ice

The winter wind howls. It's too cold for you to stay long at your square. No matter: There isn't much to see. The pond really *is* quiet. And it is covered with ice.

Touch the ice. It feels hard, but it's not hard enough. The pond is frozen over. It is not frozen solid. That's why you must NEVER walk or skate on it.

A pond doesn't freeze from the bottom up. If it did, just about everything in it would die. Instead, ice forms as a thin layer over the surface. This layer shields the water below from frigid air and winter storms. The water below cools almost to freezing but doesn't turn into ice. That's dangerously cold for people. However, most fishes can stand it, even though the cold slows them down.

When the ice melts, you may see water insects and other animals that look dead. They do not move or eat. Neither do the frogs and turtles buried in the mud. All these creatures spend winter in a deep sleep. They hardly breathe and their hearts barely beat. The little energy they need comes from stored body fat. They remain only just alive until the pond rewarms and the spring sun shines on your small square.

hat is left of the water
y lives on stored food.

Water lily

Rise and Fall

Whenever you visit your square, dip an inexpensive all-weather thermometer into the water for a minute or two and record the temperature in your notebook. In winter, if the pond isn't frozen, how cold is the water? How warm is the water when your square is bursting with life?

Think Twice

At home pour about an inch of water into a small plastic container. Place it in the freezer for an hour, then remove it. How much ice has formed? Where? When liquid water turns to ice, it expands and takes up more space. Ice is lighter than liquid water and it floats.

Ask an adult to help you break through the layer of ice in your container with the eraser end of a pencil. Drop a pea or bean into the hole. Is it easy to reach once it is under the ice? Think twice before stepping on pond ice. Remember the pea or bean, and NEVER do it.

Back to Life

The snow and ice are gone. Days are longer and warmer. Signs of spring greet you on the way to the pond: Buds are bursting open. Flowers are in bloom. Birds are singing their mating songs.

Yet at the pond not much is stirring. The water still feels quite cold. It may be spring on the calendar, but don't expect your square to spring back to life all at once. Nature has another plan, which you can watch unfold.

Look around. Perhaps a red-winged blackbird has flown in to claim your square as his. Or maybe leaves are starting to grow. Each living thing will appear when it senses it has the best chance of making a living again. For some that will be when the air or water is warmer. For others when days are longer or nights not as cold.

Make a list in your notebook of all the plants and animals you saw in your square last summer. Then mark down the date and time you see or hear them for the first time in spring. How long before water striders skate after insects or lilies sprout? When do turtles and frogs awaken and dig themselves out of the mud?

By the time you no longer need a jacket, a great blue heron may be spearing fishes in your square. Once more the whir of dragonfly wings will buzz in your ears. And the clumps of frog and snail eggs in the water are proof that nature's plan has indeed worked: The pond is back to life.

What's that smell? Rotten meat? Skunk? No. Skunk cabbage. The plant's foul odor attracts flies to carry its pollen.

Fishes that spent the winter in deeper water swim back to your square to mate and lay eggs.

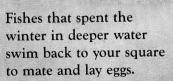

The wren has his work cut out for him. He must build a nest to attract a female.

Some birds just visit your pond on the way to their summer homes. Others stay until autumn.

It's frog season again. Never take frog eggs or tadpoles home. They belong in the pond. You don't want to harm them.

Come and get it! When warm weather returns, algae multiply quickly. Algae eaters grow and multiply too. Soon the pond is restocked with food.

35

A Pond for All Seasons

Take a shoebox and turn it so the open side faces you. Cut a hole in the top as shown. Stretch clear plastic wrap over half the hole and tape in place as shown.

Draw and color pond plants and animals, each with a flap at the top or bottom. Cut out each one, bend its flap, and tape it to the box depending on where that plant or animal lives in the pond. Tape surface-film animals to the top or bottom of the plastic wrap. Tape plants that grow out of the water to the box bottom, then pull the stems through the open half of the hole. Tape frogs, bees, and dragonflies to stems, lily pads, or flowers. Hang fishes and water bugs from strings taped to the plastic wrap. Create a new diorama for each season.

Something New

As you get older, try to keep visiting your small square. There will always be something new for you to discover about the workings of a pond.

With each passing year, notice how the pond changes. More and more plants invade the open water. There is more mud too, because the plant roots trap so much more silt and dirt. The pond cleanup crew and recycling team no longer can handle all of the dead plant parts. What remains settles on the bottom and builds up. Over time the bottom muck thickens into soil.

Eventually the plants take over. Your small square fills in with soil. So does the rest of the pond. It turns into something new—a marshy meadow.

You may have grandchildren before this happens. In the meantime, you can help keep your pond alive by never throwing trash or anything harmful into the water and never adding animals or plants that do not belong.

So smile the next time you hear people say, "Not much happens at a pond." Then tell them about your small square.

Largemouth bass

Pickerel frog

Bullhead

Banded water snake

Sponge

Water lily

What's Living in a Pond?

Can you match each living thing with its outline?

Cattail

Marsh wren

Arum

Painted turtle

Red-eared turtle

Pumpkinseed

Bluegill

Mudminnows

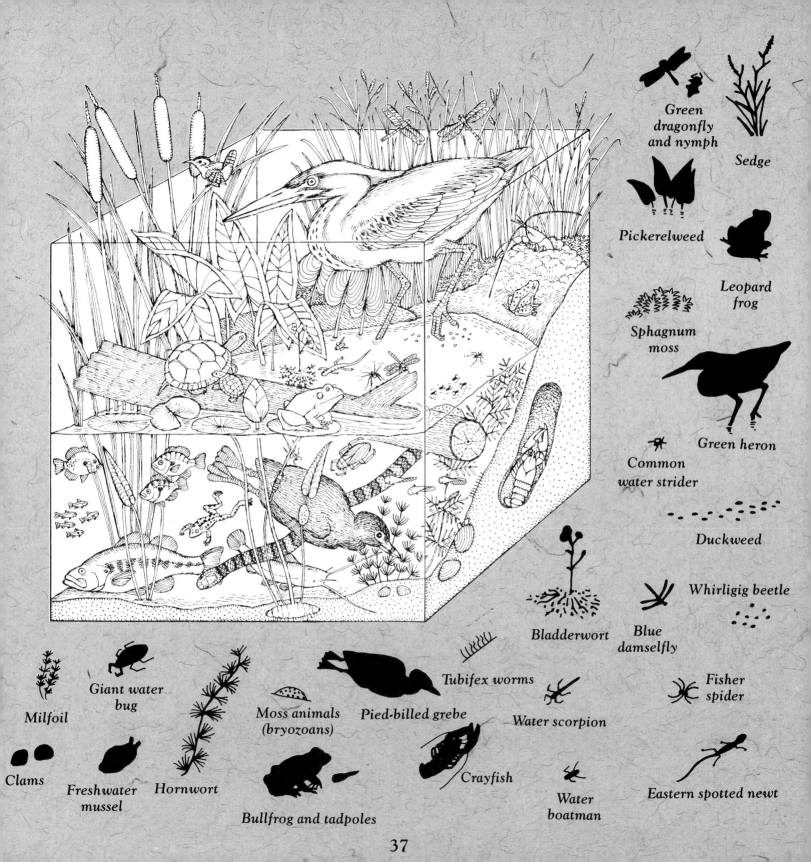

Green dragonfly and nymph

Sedge

Pickerelweed

Leopard frog

Sphagnum moss

Green heron

Common water strider

Duckweed

Whirligig beetle

Bladderwort

Blue damselfly

Milfoil

Giant water bug

Moss animals (bryozoans)

Pied-billed grebe

Tubifex worms

Water scorpion

Fisher spider

Clams

Freshwater mussel

Hornwort

Bullfrog and tadpoles

Crayfish

Water boatman

Eastern spotted newt

Many pond dwellers and pond visitors are vertebrates —animals with backbones. They include most of the big animals you will see in your square.

Look for fur on mammals, feathers on birds, and scales on reptiles and most fishes. Amphibians have thin, moist skin.

Birds

Kingfisher

Bittern

Canada goose

Green heron

Barred owl

Waterthrush

Black-crowned night heron

Yellow warbler

Wood duck

Pied-billed grebe

Red-winged blackbird

Great blue heron

Mallard duck

Mammals

Raccoon

Muskrat

Water shrew

Red bat

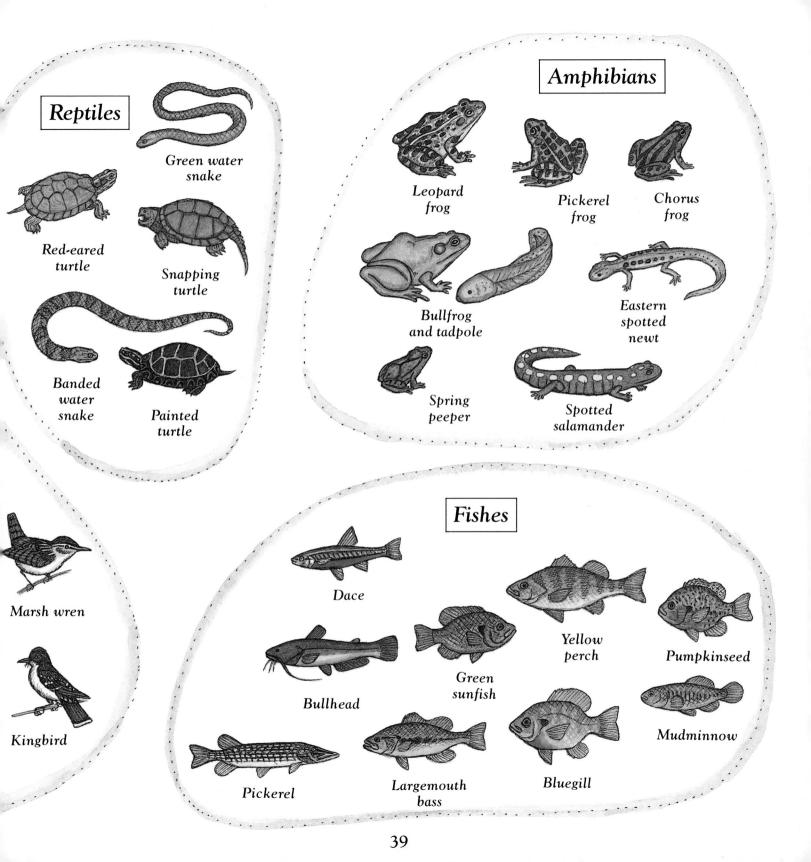

Reptiles

Green water
snake

Red-eared
turtle

Snapping
turtle

Banded
water
snake

Painted
turtle

Amphibians

Leopard
frog

Pickerel
frog

Chorus
frog

Bullfrog
and tadpole

Eastern
spotted
newt

Spring
peeper

Spotted
salamander

Marsh wren

Kingbird

Fishes

Dace

Bullhead

Green
sunfish

Yellow
perch

Pumpkinseed

Mudminnow

Pickerel

Largemouth
bass

Bluegill

These pond animals are invertebrates—they have no bones. Most are small and spend all or part of their lives in the water. For this reason you may see some of these animals as eggs, larvas, pupas, and adults.

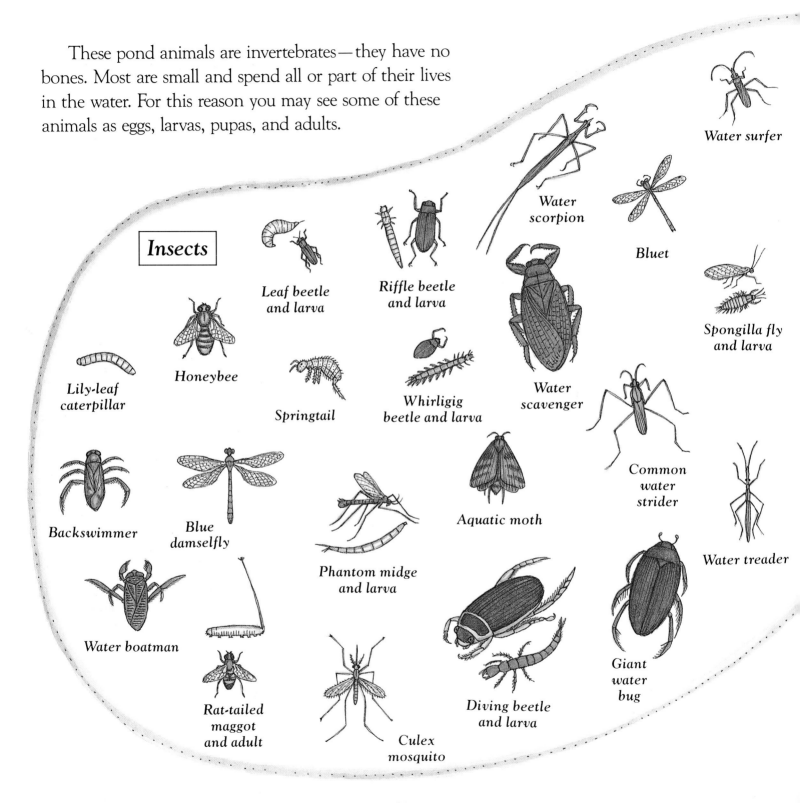

Insects

Water surfer

Water scorpion

Bluet

Leaf beetle and larva

Riffle beetle and larva

Spongilla fly and larva

Honeybee

Water scavenger

Lily-leaf caterpillar

Springtail

Whirligig beetle and larva

Common water strider

Backswimmer

Blue damselfly

Aquatic moth

Water treader

Phantom midge and larva

Water boatman

Rat-tailed maggot and adult

Culex mosquito

Diving beetle and larva

Giant water bug

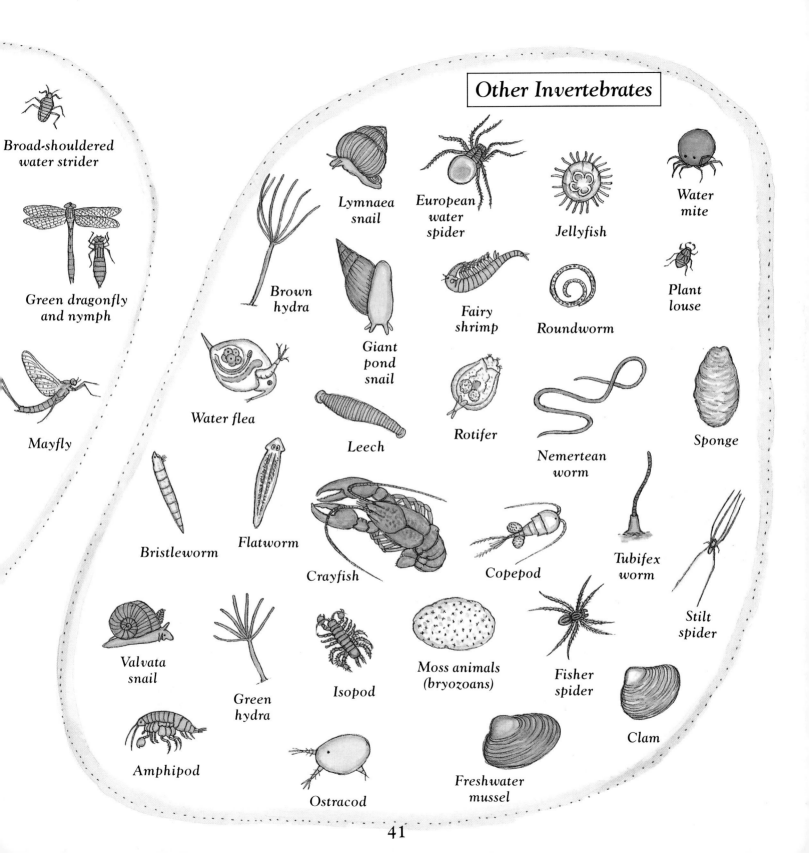

Broad-shouldered
water strider

Green dragonfly
and nymph

Mayfly

Brown
hydra

Lymnaea
snail

European
water
spider

Jellyfish

Water
mite

Giant
pond
snail

Fairy
shrimp

Roundworm

Plant
louse

Water flea

Leech

Rotifer

Nemertean
worm

Sponge

Bristleworm

Flatworm

Crayfish

Copepod

Tubifex
worm

Stilt
spider

Valvata
snail

Green
hydra

Isopod

Moss animals
(bryozoans)

Fisher
spider

Clam

Amphipod

Ostracod

Freshwater
mussel

41

Here are food makers, including plants and algae. Here also are funguses, protists, and monera that help make up the pond's cleanup crew and recycling team. And here is some of the other pond life you would need a microscope to see.

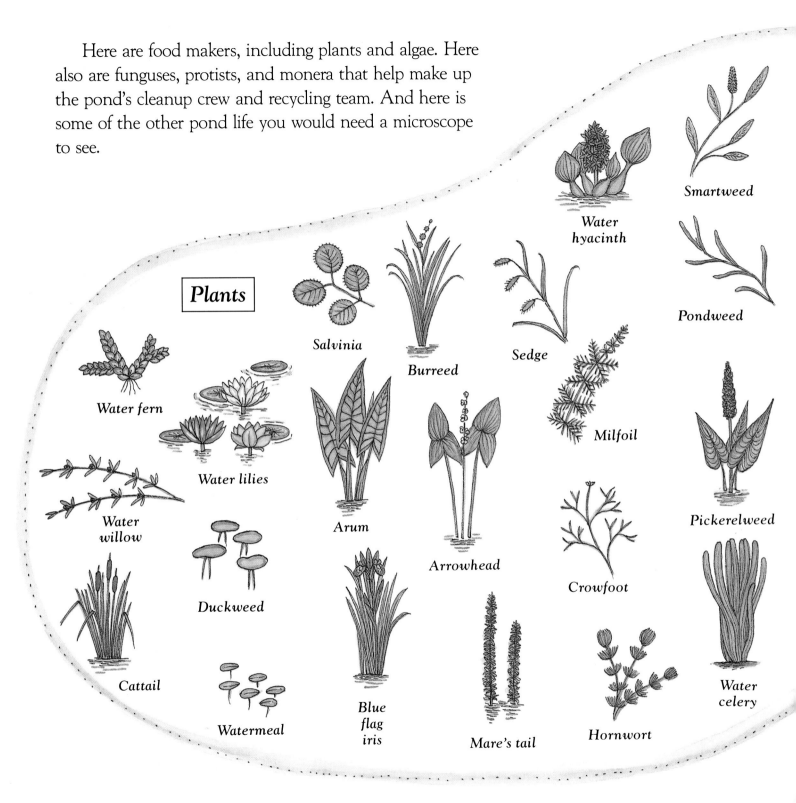

Plants

Water hyacinth

Smartweed

Pondweed

Water fern

Salvinia

Burreed

Sedge

Milfoil

Water lilies

Water willow

Arum

Arrowhead

Crowfoot

Pickerelweed

Duckweed

Cattail

Watermeal

Blue flag iris

Mare's tail

Hornwort

Water celery

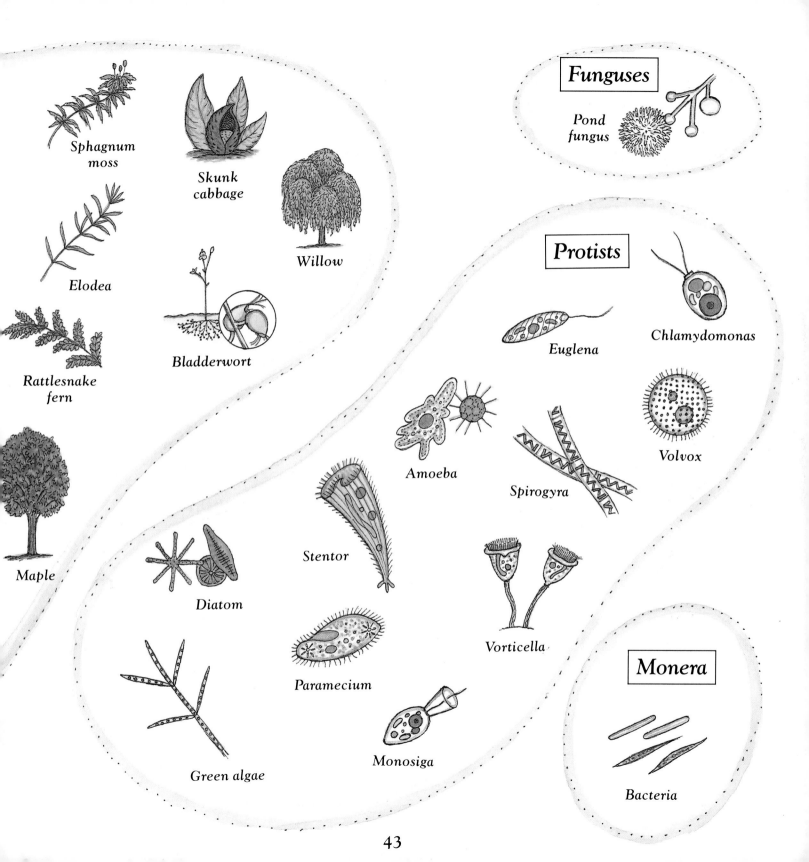

Sphagnum moss

Skunk cabbage

Willow

Elodea

Bladderwort

Rattlesnake fern

Maple

Funguses

Pond fungus

Protists

Euglena

Chlamydomonas

Amoeba

Spirogyra

Volvox

Stentor

Vorticella

Diatom

Paramecium

Green algae

Monosiga

Monera

Bacteria

Index

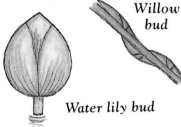

Willow bud

Water lily bud

Spring peepers in the mud

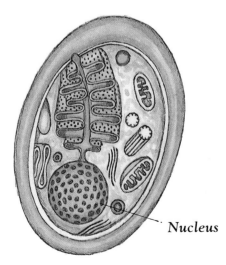

Nucleus

Foot out

Side view

Index

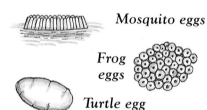
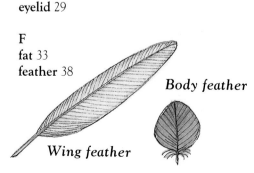
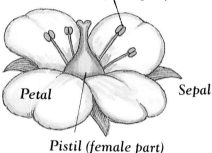

Index

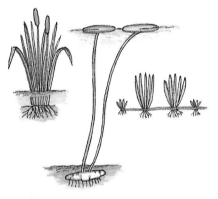

Index

rotifer 30

S
scale 38
seed 11
shell 19, 23
shore 6, 11
shrew 29
silt 27, 36
skin 10, 38
skunk cabbage 34
snail 15, 17, 21, 23, 34
snow 34
soil 27, 36
sperm 24. *A male reproductive cell.*

Nucleus

Frog sperm

spider 10, 12, 13, 29
sponge 17, 23, 24, 30
spring 9, 30, 33, 34
spring peeper 29
springtail 12, 13
stem 7, 10, 16, 19, 23, 25, 31, 36
stinging cell 14

storm 33
summer 9, 27, 29, 30, 31, 34
sun 10, 15, 17, 18, 19, 25, 29, 31, 33, 35
sunfish 24, 25
surface film 12–15, 21

T
tadpole 3, 21, 23, 35
tail 16
teeth 23
temperature 33
tentacle (TEN-tuh-kul) 14
thermometer 33
tongue 17
tracks 9
tree 29
tunnel 29
turtle 3, 13, 19, 20, 22, 26, 31, 33, 34
twilight 29

V
vertebrate 38

W
water boatman 15
water bug 14, 17, 21
water flea 15, 19

water lily 17, 19, 25, 29, 33, 34. *See also* lily pad.

water mite 17
water scorpion 15
water snake 13
water spider 20
water strider 12, 13, 32, 34
water tiger 22
water willow 11, 30
web 10, 12, 20
wind 11, 17, 27, 33
wing 3, 15, 34
winter 9, 25, 30, 31, 32, 33, 34
worm 17, 24, 27
wren 10, 35

Further Reading

To find out more, look for the following in a library or bookstore:

Golden Guides, Golden Press, New York, NY

Golden Field Guides, Golden Press, New York, NY

The Audubon Society Beginner Guides, Random House, New York, NY

The Audubon Society Field Guides, Alfred A. Knopf, New York, NY

The Peterson Field Guides, Houghton Mifflin Co., Boston, MA

Reader's Digest North American Wildlife, Reader's Digest, Pleasantville, NY

Eyewitness Books, Alfred A. Knopf, New York, NY

Look Closer: Pond Life, Dorling Kindersley, New York, NY

Look in an art supply store or in the library for books on how to draw plants and animals. If you like to sketch and paint outdoors, here are some things you'll find handy:

- paper
- number 2 pencil
- paintbrush
- bottle of black ink
- black drawing pen
- tray of watercolors
- eraser
- plastic bottle for water
- stiff cardboard or clipboard to draw on